HOW TO

READ A COW

AND OTHER ESSENTIAL

LIFE LESSONS

Warren V. Hunt

WARREN V. HUNT

ISBN:1939331137

ISBN-978-1-939331-13-7:

Some of these stories were first printed in

Western Ag Reporter.

CONTENTS

INTRODUCTION

This collection of stories is but a few of dozens that my father has told over the years about growing up on a cattle ranch. As you'll find out below, his father (my grandfather) had homesteaded in the early twentieth century. When I visited the old ranch with my father in the 1970s, it was still out in the middle of nowhere, sixty miles from Gillette, Wyoming.

Dad is now 92 years old and still firing on all cylinders. He never tires of telling these stories. They have a different quality when written than when he tells them over coffee. He obviously delights in his use of language and humor. They're mostly stories about a vanished way of life that he saw the tail end of as a boy. But of course, there is something universal about them, which is why we love to read them.

Dad is a technophile and has recently been assisting me with the publication of public domain books for e-readers. He even bought himself a Kindle. So I thought it was high time to bring his stories to the ebook public and to print-on-demand. We hope you enjoy these stories as much as we do. If you do, please be sure to write a review on the retail site where you purchased this book. Who knows? Maybe we'll get him to come up with Volume II.

BRIAN V. HUNT

WARREN V. HUNT

NEXT TIME MAKE SURE THE CINCH IS TIGHT

saying is just a collection of words that never made it into the big league of proverbs and axioms. A saying may be a bush league sentence but it has application to a wide range of subjects. One such saying in our family grew out of a string of incidents which caused me some degree of chagrin and embarrassment over the years. The first such incident occurred as I prepared to attend first grade at our rural school.

It was eleven miles to my country school house by road but it was only five miles to the school house if I went out our southeast gate, through Bruce Hamlin's horse pasture on Bower Creek, over Tarbell Ridge and through the northwest gate of the school section land. The most logical way to traverse that terrain was by horseback.

The horse I rode to school in first grade was named Johnny. He was a calm, quiet, steady old bay and we often called him "Old Johnny." He was too darned lazy to buck which probably led my parents to assign him to me for my first grade school transportation. The first time I put a saddle on Johnny it was struggle to get it up there but I made it. But when I started to climb aboard, that saddle slowly rotated over on Johnny's left side and hung there above my red face.

As you people know, a cinch is an appendage to a riding saddle that encircles the horse's belly. Its purpose is to affix the saddle to the horse in a firm and solid manner such that you, the saddle and the horse became a cohesive entity for whatever gyrations you may collectively encounter later. Apparently I had failed to meet some portion of that description as I tried to saddle Old Johnny. But salvation and furtherance of my education was close at hand.

Uncle Happy had observed my efforts to saddle Old Johnny. Furthermore, Uncle Happy knew that Old Johnny had a sneaky corner in his brain. What Old Johnny had done just as I reached for the cinch ring was to slowly and almost invisibly inhale until his chest was about twice its normal size. As soon as I dropped the stirrup he exhaled and shrunk back to normal size. I now had a loose cinch and a wobbly saddle.

Uncle Happy walked over beside Old Johnny and gave him a pat on the neck. That was also a sneaky and misleading gesture as Johnny soon found out. Uncle Happy quickly pulled up his knee to hit Johnny in the belly with the force of a large sledge hammer. While Old Johnny was all doubled up gasping for air, Uncle Happy quickly pulled the slack out of my cinch and I now had a solid saddle—and a somewhat breathless horse—on which to take off for school. As I rode off, Uncle Happy said quietly, "Next time, make sure the cinch is tight."

At my size in first grade, I couldn't belt Old Johnny hard enough to knock the wind out of him like Uncle Happy did. So I used Johnny's own devious psychology. I would run the latigo strap through the cinch ring and snug it up just a bit. Sure enough, that old devil would turn into a balloon. I would just wait a while and then wait some more. Now if an old bay horse could turn purple he must have done so as he stood there holding his breath. He would finally have to give up that idea if he wanted to keep on living. As he let go with a big swoosh of air, I would finish tightening the cinch and away we would go with a snug saddle.

A few years older and several inches taller I got my first job away from the ranch. A neighboring rancher, Roy Greer, hired me to "break" a string of broncs for him. Roy apparently had noticed the canny way in which I outwitted Old Johnny earlier.

Roy was a pretty good judge of horses when it came to their personality and poise. He never said anything about my work except when I was saddling up a critter that he knew had a rather unpleasant disposition. He would walk over and lean on the corral fence and watch for a while. Then he would make a quiet remark to me which I knew contained much more friendly advice than the mere words indicated. Upon hearing his remark I checked all my rigging again, perhaps changed to a spade bit, tightened my own belt, pulled my hat down another quarter of an inch and climbed aboard. What Roy said to me was, "Next time, make sure the cinch is tight."

Along about this same time in my budding career as a ranch hand I became friends with Dean Miller, a neighboring ranch hand about my age. Dean was quite handy with a saddle rope. I wasn't very good at this effort but nevertheless we used to team up in some of the local rodeos for the calf roping contests.

We did not enter those contests for the prize money—it usually wouldn't buy a good saddle blanket—even a used one. I think rather that it was probably to garner some of the illogical attention lavished upon rodeo contestants by those beautiful cowgirls in their tight fittin' jeans.

Came a day I was roping and Dean was hazing. Everything started off right. I laid my loop over that calf's neck so neat and quick that I was sure I was headed for the winner's prize. While I was gloating over my great skill, that calf hit the end of my rope. Evidently I had paid more attention to some tight fittin' jeans than I had to my rigging since my saddle started to stand right up on its front end. Then it started to rotate sideways.

Knowing the battle was lost, I threw my dally from the saddle horn, kicked the saddle up straight and shuddered to a stop. It was bad enough to know that I had done the unpardonable by letting that calf get away with my rope. That's like a gunfighter shooting himself in the foot. Dean then compounded the situation even further for me by sidling his horse up to mine right there in that big arena in front of all those cowgirls in their tight fittin' jeans and saying "Next time, make sure the cinch is tight".

Shortly thereafter, I left ranch life to explore other possibilities which I thought had less chance of bodily harm, more glamour and greater pay. Learning to fly an airplane was one of those activities, which some people would say isn't much of an improvement over riding broncs. Russ Halley was my flight instructor. He owned and operated a flying school in what used to be his cow pasture in South Dakota. In fact, he still kept a few cattle on his grass-covered airport which sometime led to interesting problems in planning a landing approach. There came a time in the series of my flying lessons when Russ and I went up to perform acrobatic flight which was then required of fledgling airmen.

Contrary to popular opinion, most acrobatic maneuvers do not tend to throw you out of the airplane—if they are done with proper planning and execution. That day, however, I failed to properly plan and execute a simple loop. Right at the top of a loop with the airplane, and us, upside down, I fell away from the seat. Luckily I did not have to use my parachute as the seat belt and shoulder harness snapped me up short after what seemed an eternity of falling. My feet came off the rudder pedals and we fell off in a tailspin and dropped 1400 feet in rather quick order. I subsequently got myself glued back to the seat and landed the airplane in Russ' pasture without hitting any of his cows. I fully expected my aviation career to end right then and there. Instead, Russ came over and put his hand on my shoulder and said, "Next time, make sure the cinch is tight".

A few years ago, my wife and I checked into a nice hotel in Salt Lake City. Unlike the old ranch buildings, this hotel had an indoor privy. That bathroom looked pretty much like others I had seen in other hotels. But it contained one treacherous device which I had never encountered before. At first glance, this deceiving device looked just like any other of its kind with a glossy white exterior. What it was, was a foam rubber toilet seat.

In the interest of modesty, I will not describe all of the details of what happened next. Just enough so that you will be forewarned should you encounter this devious gadget in some of your travels. I know it was invented by some well-meaning individual. I also know the inventor had never had any experiences which would give him an appreciation of a tight cinch and snug saddle.

Just as I became comfortable on that cushy little throne, the left side of the foam rubber seat collapsed. Instantly, my mind cranked back many years to the instinctive reaction of my ranch training days. I "grabbed for leather." Only there wasn't any handy. Instead it was the shower curtain. The shower curtain, curtain rod and all its attendant paraphernalia crashed into the bathtub with accompanying audible fanfare. Then that invention of the devil immediately struck again. The right side now collapsed with a swoosh like a tire going flat. This time, my attempts to "stay in the saddle," so to speak, resulted in the paper roller being torn from the wall. Had I been wearing spurs, there would have been a pile of chipped porcelain among the debris.

As I contemplated the wreckage in that small room and tried to get my heartbeat back to normal, I heard my wife yelling from the adjacent room in an unnecessarily loud manner mixed with hysterical hilarity, "Next time, make sure the cinch is tight."

HOW TO READ A COW

Over the years, many disputes have arisen over the subject of how to read a cow. Men have been hung for failure to properly read a cow or, more accurately, for trying to change the writing on a cow. Many western states have statutes that require writing on a cow. There are thousands of government employees in the western states whose job is to read cows.

What we are talking about here is the type of writing, commonly called a brand, which is applied with a very hot iron. Brands have been applied to pottery, animals, women and slaves for thousands of years. Being a bit of a social coward, I am going to ride around the purpose and merits of most of those applications and limit myself here to the subject of brands on cattle.

The purpose of branding is to show ownership of the animal in a rather permanent way. That sounds rather simple but let us look at some potential pitfalls in that process.

The clearest way to indicate ownership of an object or animal is to write your name on it. That does not create much work for Don Ho but it is a different ball game for Jeremiah Michael McGillicuddy. It takes quite a while to write Jeremiah Michael McGillicuddy with a pencil and considerably longer if you are dancing around with a hot piece of iron in your hand trying to inscribe it on a wriggling animal. Besides, if Mac tried to use his full name as his brand, he would have nothing but roast cow when he got through with the job.

Which leads us to the first rule of brand design, "Don't cook the critter."

In order to conform to the first rule of branding and to avoid unnecessary work, cattle owners resorted to using their initials to form their brand. So Tom Jackson started using TJ. That presented a problem for Ted Jones when he started his herd on a ranch about ten miles from Tom's place. Ted, by golly, insisted on using his initials but with a little different twist accomplished by putting a bar between the letters so it read "T—J" (T Bar J).

As time went on, it developed that the T—J owner, Ted Jones, had an active imagination and a keen sense of artistry. He noted that some of the cattle branded with his neighbor's TJ brand had quite a bit of space between the T and the J (T J) into which a bar would fit nicely to convert it into a T—J. He tried out that idea one dark evening and found that it worked well with the result that his herd began to grow at rate suggesting that all his cows were giving birth to triplets—a bovine improbability. This forgery of cow writing is called "running a brand" and was definitely frowned upon by the local sheriff and, of course, the true owner of the animal should he have occasion to discover the nefarious practice.

This practice led to the second rule of brand design, "Confuse the counterfeiters."

Brand designers came up with a number of innovations to complicate brand-running while still leaving open the option of using initials. Should use of the owner's initials still be his heart's desire, the letters were often modified to be lazy, tumbling, connected, reversed, or flying. Other spacers and modifiers were added like slashes, bars, quarter-circles or full circles. These could be placed in various positions relative to the letters including before, above, between, under, after or around the letters themselves.

All of the widgets and gidgets on brands created another problem. Can you imagine, "Quarter-circle, tumbling B, lazy D connected" for a brand.

Result—the third rule—"It must trip lightly off the tongue."

During a spell of low cattle prices back in the 20's and 30's, a number of ranch owners put up some log cabins near the main ranch house and called their operation a working dude ranch. You can be assured that the Quarter-circle, tumbling B, Lazy D-connected Ranch did not make it. Its euphonic complexity and that B stumbling around in the middle of all that other garbage just plain made it a loser. But the Flying W Ranch name, with its wings of flight, conjured up images of white gossamer clouds floating through an azure sky, moonlight romance under a whispering pine by the shores of a sparkling lake and cool breezes wafting down from the snow tipped mountains nearby. Guess which dude ranch the New York City secretary or Minneapolis bank clerk picked for their summer vacation.

Once brands started packing around all that paraphernalia, they began to look like jigsaw puzzles to brand-illiterate people. So you will not be embarrassed by being accused of being a brand-illiterate person, should you take your next vacation at the Flying W Ranch or visit your ranching cousin in Montana, let me give you the rather simple rules for reading brands.

Left-to-right — top-to-bottom — outside-in. Just plug in the modifiers as you go.

Most people can handle left-to-right with fair comfort. They sometimes get a little mixed up with top-to-bottom. If they are going to stub their toe, it is generally with outside-in. Should you have trouble with that one while in a city environment, just remember that one of your local convenience stores is the "Circle K"—not the "K Circle." That chain, by the way, grew out of a little store a Mrs. Kay operated in Texas along about 1951, a circumstance of location and ownership which probably led to the brand logo. Check the big logo on the building sometime when you drive by one of their stores just in case you don't have a cow to practice on.

Back when I was assigned duties as a branding fire-tender and calf-wrestler as a young lad on the ranch, I could read brands with no problem but I did not know all those fancy rules I just spelled out for you. Later on when I got a bit smarter and more curious, I asked Dad why he picked the Quarter-Circle Lazy D A brand.

It sure did not match any of his VLH initials. It required four different irons to emboss it onto an animal thus requiring several trips between the fire and the supine beast. If you had tried to put that brand on an animal with a one-piece stamp iron, it would have violated the first rule I gave you about cooking the poor critter.

However, it certainly was a counterfeit confounder and, so far as I know, Dad never had to hang anybody or have them incarcerated for such shady activity.\

As I waited for Dad's answer to my question regarding his Quarter-Circle Lazy D A brand, I was expecting a story on some deep ranch secret, a hidden code or a romantic tale of an early love. Alas, such was not my luck.

Dad answered, "I liked the sound of it."

Oh well, two out of three isn't bad—it does trip lightly off the tongue.

AN EQUINE TANGO

One thousand hooves of 250 cows, calves, steers and heifers gathered in a dry meadow on a late summer day stirred up a fair cloud of dust as the animals milled about making cow talk with each other. The heifers and steers weren't saying much but the plaintive cry of calves accidentally separated from their mothers during the confusion of travel and the much lower-toned answer of the cows seeped out of the dust cloud. As the riders circled the herd to hold it in place the noise decreased as cows found their calves and a few animals even lay down to rest after their sometimes strenuous trek of the morning.

Beginning shortly after sunrise, Dad and I, along with the help of three neighbors, had rousted these animals out of the hills, gullies and valleys of the Quarter-Circle Lazy DA summer pasture and drifted them into this meadow two miles north of the main ranch buildings and corrals. The objective of this roundup was to sort out the yearling steers and move them to another pasture with better grass and some alfalfa stubble that would put a bit of fat on their ribs before they were shipped off to market later in the fall. Weight and sleekness counted when a rancher and a cattle buyer began dickering about price.

At this point in the proceedings we were faced with a logistical planning decision. Believe it or not, ranchers often have to make logistical planning decisions even though you might think only officials of big corporations make decisions with such big words in front of them.

The easiest location in which to sort cattle is a corral, particularly if it is provided with sorting gates which can be swung back and forth to direct steers in one direction and other animals in another direction. However, we were two miles from our corral with three narrow intervening wire gates through which we would have to squeeze the herd. After the steers were sorted out of the group, the cows, calves and heifers would have to be driven right back through those same wire gates to our present location. Based on his knowledge of those obstacles, Dad's logistical planning decision was that we would stay right where we were in the dry meadow and do a "range cut".

During a range cut, a few of the riders are assigned to keep the bulk of the herd in one location and encourage the cutouts to stay in a holding area. The cow cuttin' riders slowly move into the herd until they find an animal to be cut out and slowly and calmly push it out of the herd to a holding area. In this case, Dad assigned the three neighbor men to be the holder riders and decreed that he and I would be the cutting riders. That was the neighborly thing to do as the holders had a rather relaxing effort coming while Dad and I were going to work up a sweat—or at least our horses would.

Right away, I knew I had made the wrong choice that morning when I selected my pinto mare, Little Lady, for my horse *du jour*. I had done some training with Little Lady in the art of cow cutting but she still carried a student classification in that department of ranch affairs. I now knew that I should have picked my favorite saddle horse, Lady, since she and I had already done quite a bit of cow cutting training and work over the past couple of years with the result that she was an expert in that field of endeavor.

A real expert cow cutting mare like Lady is a thing of beauty to watch in operation. You could ride Lady into a herd of cattle, point her nose at a particular animal you wanted to remove from the bunch and then drop the reins. From there on she knew what needed to be done with no further instructions. She would slowly and gracefully do that equine terpsichorean act required of a successful cow cutting horse. That would involve a bit of waltzing, a slow fox-trot, or a tango with a smidgen of a cha-cha thrown in for good measure. She would take the animal out of the herd even walking sideways if necessary, one front leg crossing over the other, to keep the animal moving toward the chosen holding point.

Only slow dances may be used in a cow cutting. The affair generally starts out with eye contact between the horse and the chosen cow and perhaps even a slight bow of recognition followed by a few waltz steps. The pace then picks up as both animals go into a rumba rhythm with the horse guiding the cow away from the crowded space near the main herd to allow more room for the intricate steps to follow. Apparently the cow becomes embarrassed out there in the open and tries to sashay around the horse to rejoin her watching friends. The horse then insists on the toe-tingling taps of a tango as they glide back and forth as well as left and right on the grass covered dance floor. Finally, the cow heads for the holding area at a fast fox-trot in order to get out of the limelight and the dance is over. The horse and rider, each wearing a satisfied smile, move back to the main herd to select another dancing partner.

A dance fatal to the success of a cow cutting episode is the jitter-bug. Invariably the cow darts out of a jitterbug twirl to run around the horse and successfully rejoin her observing friends and relatives. Should the cow use this sneaky procedure to escape from her horse partner the horse must stop in place with a scornful look of scorn and disapproval upon its face until the cow resumes a more sedate step.

This explanation of a rare skill refers to a "cow" but the same rules apply when the cutting horse is dancing with a steer, heifer, or calf.

To sort the steers out of that herd we proceeded to do the job backwards by some standards—we first cut out the cows, calves and heifers to leave the steers by themselves. The reason for that apparently illogical process has to do with the diverse personality of members of the herd. Steers have a great propensity for going into jitterbug mode when dancing with a cutting horse with many end-runs back to the main group. This causes a great loss of time and effort.

Rather than further malign the personality of steers, let me tell you about a few traits of the cows.

Those cows have been around the ranch long enough to have acquired some understanding and respect for the steering signals projected by a horse and rider. During the cow's younger years, it is likely that some of that understanding and respect was engendered by a stinging reminder from the end of a blacksnake whip or saddle rope should she be so foolish as to ignore the instructions being given her. As a result of all that history, a cow just naturally requires less persuasion to be directed to a specified area.

If a cowhand is doing at least half of what he is supposed to be doing during a gather of cattle, he will have taken care to identify the natural leader of a clan of livestock as they are collected from the range pasture. In a mixed herd of cows and younger stock, the leader will generally be one of the big mommas. So when you get ready to sort the herd, you first cut out the natural leader big mommas whenever you have a choice. After all, they are used to being out front without any embarrassment or chagrin on their part and so will take your sorting cue in a much more graceful and polite manner than one of the underlings of the clan.

Most of the time the strong familial attraction between mother and offspring will cause a calf to drift right along with momma. When that happens, you have two for the price of one.

Somewhat like their human counterparts, the young heifers seem to have a more genteel and docile attitude toward strenuous physical activity. Therefore, they are not too difficult to cut out and push over with the cows and calves.

About the time all but a few of the heifers had traipsed across the meadow to join the cows, a couple of the steers would take note of what was happening. Hey Mac, most of the girls have left us. Word of this unsatisfactory state of affairs would quickly spread among the steers. They would then collectively launch an effort to get over to the corner of the meadow where the heifers were now located. This required two-thirds of the riders had to turn their direction of attack and hold the steers back while the remaining riders sorted out the last of the heifers. Being anatomically deficient, those steers could not engage in any late nights on the couch with the heifers but they still liked to socialize with them.

I meandered over to a clump of sagebrush with Little Lady where I reviewed the rules and regulations of cow cutting with her. I also made the logistical planning decision that Little Lady and I would first sort out only cows because of their expected tendency to favor the waltz type of dance. With that choice, Little Lady displayed mediocre, but tolerable performance. However, when most of the cows were sorted out with little choice but to cut out a heifer, my pinto pony began to exhibit tendencies with eventually led to our downfall in the full sense of the word. She began to louse up her choice of dances.

The heifer and Little Lady properly started out with the specified waltz steps. Once out of the herd, that vain little heifer decided to show off for the crowd by going into an energetic jitterbug. Instead of scowling, Little Lady started to jitterbug as well. The sight of a jitterbugging pinto so frightened the heifer that she broke into a fast trot across the meadow quickly followed by my amateur cutting horse despite my previous warnings against such a silly response. I was about to blow the whistle on Little Lady's play when events took a rapid turn for the worse. Little Lady stepped in a prairie dog hole and fell.

The first thing you want to do when parting company with a falling horse is to get your feet out of the stirrups. I accomplished that task with great alacrity. The second thing you want to do is get whichever leg is on the down side of the animal elevated and try to get your whole body on what will finally be the "up-side" of the horse. As you can imagine, 800 to 1200 pounds of horse laying on, or rolling on, your leg can cause considerable discomfort and perhaps a parting of your femur which will sure inhibit your tango.

I managed to avoid that unpleasant possibility, as well. However, I was trapped by one of Newton's laws which says a body in motion tends to stay in motion. So I was propelled forward along our path of travel with such velocity that I skidded along on my right side for about twenty feet stirring up a new cloud of dust. That would not have been so bad except for the fact the ground I traversed in that embarrassing horizontal position was liberally strewn with leaf cactus. When I managed to get myself into a standing position, I found that I had collected a fair sized crop of cactus in the flesh of my right side from ankle to shoulder. My clothing was literally nailed to my skin by cactus thorns.

My story of standing there with all that cactus perforating my epidermis likely evokes in you not one iota of sympathy or compassion for me. But I'll bet you are getting all teary-eyed picturing poor Little Lady lying on the ground with a broken leg requiring her to be sent to the big Horse Heaven in the sky like in the old western movies. Almost to my dismay, she did not break a leg and scrambled to her feet without one single cactus spine in her hide. I did fling a collection of verbal darts in her direction characterized by as much invective as I could master at that young age.

My barbs probably did not hurt Little Lady very much but they sure made me feel better.

I gave her an F for the day's lesson then flunked her completely out of my Cow Cuttin' 201 class.

MY BUFFALO HUNT

Should you be lucky enough to become a visitor at a present-day cattle ranch in Wyoming you will probably discover a fair collection of firearms about the place. While only a minority of ranchers are members of the National Rifle Association, they will quickly turn various shades of red or purple if you should make the mistake of expounding strong views in favor of gun registration and control. If you compound your social error by failing to take heed of the Technicolor display on their faces and continue your argument in favor of tampering with their right to bear arms by free and unfettered choice, you may be invited to leave the premises promptly and rapidly. On a bad day the rancher may even reinforce that invitation by a prod from the business end of one of his shooting irons.

Before you get all huffy and puffy about this apparent lack of hospitality you must consider that many ranchers in the West are descendants of settlers who came into the area in the latter part of the 19th century when the possession and use of firearms had valuable applications in the settlers quest for food and protection of life and property.

The Civil War ended in 1865 but lingering animosity between veterans of the Blue and the Gray led to gunplay for years afterward. In 1876, Custer and some 200 troopers of his Seventh Cavalry met their deaths at the hands of warriors gathered by Sitting Bull on the Little Bighorn River near what is now Hardin, Montana. Even as late as 1880 there was but an uneasy peace between the white settlers and Native American tribes. Geronimo did not surrender to General George Crook until 1886, four years after Crook went back for his second tour of duty in the Territory of Arizona. Renegade white ruffians drifted through the country rustling cattle or stealing horses and robbing travelers and banks, particularly if they suspected some of the gold from the Black Hills of South Dakota was in their possession. The diet in a portion of the western ranch homes of the late 1800's included wild game meat such as deer, antelope, bear, rabbit, or porcupine, at least part of the time. Ranchers also conducted warfare with the wolves and coyotes that preyed upon their sheep and cattle.

My grandparents were born in the late 1870's, which was about the right time for them to grow up while there was still considerable concerned conversation about the events and practices described above. As a result, they packed along various firearms as they reached adulthood and migrated by team and wagon from Iowa to their homestead in western South Dakota. Dad reinforced his gun education by charging off in a burst of patriotic fervor to join the United States Army at the time of World War I. As you can guess, I was next in line to learn gun handling techniques whether I wanted to or not.

To tell you the truth, I was not all that thrilled about learning to shoot a gun. By the time I came along in the family, most of the exciting reasons my grandparents had owned guns had disappeared. There were no angry Indians skulking around the hills on our ranch. In fact, the first Indians I ever saw were getting even with the palefaces by taking their money to put on trick riding shows at a county fair in Sheridan, Wyoming. Mother would not sully her skillet to cook wild game steaks. Furthermore, the nearest bank was 60 miles away so there was little chance that I would be able to stop a covey of bank robbers in the course of their work.

However, Dad started me toward becoming a Wyoming gunman by giving me a Daisy air rifle when I was about nine years of age. That was the first of a string of shooting irons which came into my hands during the next twelve years as I worked my way up to a lever action repeating rifle and a 32 caliber six-shot revolver. I must admit right up front that I never did become much of a menace as a pistolero which probably made it fortunate that I did not meet up with anyone that needed shooting. My brother did work his way into that category a few times by sneaky and premature disclosure to my parents of some of my more serious scientific experiments like smoking coffee grounds down by the corral. He was saved only by the Code of the West that banned the shooting of anyone in your own family.

Once I was on my way to becoming a marksman with my new air rifle, shooting at tin cans became a pretty tame game. I began to look for more lively targets to shoot at. It was not long before I was presented with the opportunity to take a shot at a real live target with my weapon.

Dad had asked me to ride out into the northeast grazing pasture and bring back a Hereford bull that he planned to sell to a neighbor. After saddling my sorrel mare, Lady, I filled my air rifle with lead pellets and tied it across the back of my saddle with the expectation that I would run across a target more energetic than a tin can. I was absolutely certain that I could ward off an attack perpetrated by any of the dangerous animals inhabiting the pastures such as gophers, squirrels, crows, magpies, snakes or mice.

After searching through the pasture for about an hour, I found the bull which was the object of my mission. He was making amorous advances toward a young heifer at the time I spotted him which probably accounted for his reluctance to willing go along with my plan to drift him back to the main ranch buildings. However, with the help of Lady's expertise in bovine psychology we extracted him from the herd and started our homeward journey. Every quarter of a mile he would apparently recall another of the many charms of that young heifer and try an end run to head back in her direction. That tactic soon became a bit tiresome to me and was particularly frustrating because I did not have a blacksnake whip with which to emphasize my steering commands to the bull.

Then I remembered the blunderbuss I was carrying on the back of my saddle.

I jerked the tie strings loose, levered a BB into the chamber and waited for the next sashay that bull was certain to make. When he started his next escape maneuver, an unusual thing happened to that critter. A hump sprouted on his shoulders, he grew a beard, developed long scraggly hair and his horns became short and curly. I was looking at a mean buffalo. At the same time, my air rifle turned into a Sharps 52 caliber boomer.

Lady had already accepted the challenge presented and immediately pulled up beside my galloping buffalo. I looped my reins around the saddle horn, raised my buffalo rifle, aimed for a heart shot and pulled the trigger. A surprising turn of events then occurred, none of which involved that bison falling down dead.

The instant I pulled the trigger, Lady made a sharp turn to the right. The laws of inertia being what they are, I continued on straight ahead to land flat on the ground behind the departing buffalo. Hearing the thump made as my body hit the ground and the whistle as all the air left my lungs, that ugly beast came to a snorting stop and turned around to paw clouds of dust into the air while he decided what to do next.

As I lay on the ground contemplating my options I concluded that the possibility of successful completion of any of them was rather meager indeed. Shooting a bullet into that craggy forehead was one great idea considerably faulted by the fact that my buffalo gun lay on the ground at least 20 feet from me. As sanity and logic again began to return to my brain and my vision began to clear, I also noted that my Sharps 52 was turning back into an air rifle. Climbing a pine tree was a very attractive option marred only by the realization that the nearest one was four hundred yards away. I discarded the notion of getting back in the saddle again because that would require that I run right by that dusty buffalo to where Lady was nibbling grass as she calmly awaited the outcome of the current state of affairs.

I wish there was a glamorous ending to this event but I can't come up with one. As it turned out, I did absolutely nothing which led to a conclusion which was satisfactory to me. The reason I did nothing was because I did not yet have enough oxygen back in my lungs to lift an arm let alone grab my rifle, climb a tree or jump in the saddle. Dismayed by my cowardly behavior and lack of fighting spirit, my mad buffalo reverted to a calm old Hereford bull and wandered off in the direction of the heifer from which I had so impolitely separated him.

After I had inhaled enough air to become mobile again, I retrieved my puny little pea-shooter, climbed back in the saddle and again headed the bull for home. As I rode along, I mentally analyzed the previous series of events for such increase in my wisdom as it might provide. In doing so, I came across one glaring error I had made.

A good saddle horse will put up with all kinds of foolish endeavors its rider might initiate as long as the horse has some warning and education on the matter beforehand. Lady would tolerate with considerable grace a rope twirling around her or a bullwhip cracking over her head because she and I had studied on the matter and had practiced the activity previously. However, in my haste to down my buffalo, I had failed to have a conversation with Lady about any firearms to be discharged in her proximity. That led to her sudden evasive action as I pulled the trigger on my big buffalo gun. In all fairness to Lady, I must admit that I, too, would probably jump a bit if someone snuck up behind me and torched off a rifle such that the bullet screamed by my left ear.

Perhaps another moral to this story is that you should not interfere with the love life of a 1500 pound bull if you can avoid it.

READING SIGN

My sign reading talents nearly got me into trouble with Santa Claus on Christmas morning not long after my eighth birthday.

It had always puzzled me as to how Santa Claus could get into our small ranch cabin to leave presents without creating noise that would wake me up. Even if he managed to move about without causing some kind of ruckus he was bound to leave some kind of tracks or a thread of his red suit. There was just no way a guy could drive up with a herd of reindeer pulling a sled and then tromp around in the yard without leaving tracks and other sign. The door hinges on the cabin always squeaked when the door was opened or shut. The coal bucket sitting by the pot-bellied heating stove was a hazard to pedestrian traffic. Oh sure, the cookies and milk we left for Santa were always gone in the morning but that was negative evidence. Besides, I had a sneaking suspicion that Wayne, my younger brother, got away with those tasty treats most of the time anyway.

With the temperature at near 10 degrees Fahrenheit, the wind had died and snow began to fall on Christmas Eve. By the time we went to bed there was already several inches of new snow in the yard. Dawn brought a bright winter sun to make that snow sparkle like millions of diamonds. With about six inches of light, fluffy snow on the ground, I knew it was going to be a great day for reading sign when I woke up. After all, it is rather difficult for anyone or anything to move around in new, clean snow without leaving tracks. Conditions were at their best for reading Santa Claus sign.

Like most ranch children, I learned at an early age to observe the many signs which are visible around the ranch. Some of that knowledge came from natural curiosity. Some came from Dad. Much of my sign reading training came from Uncle Happy who was a skilled hunter of wild game and a trapper of coyotes and bobcats. Some said that Uncle Happy could track a fly through a raging sand storm on a dark night. I knew he was good but I was a bit skeptical about that "dark night" part. By the time I was six years of age I could identify the tracks of all the animals which might normally wander around the ranch, be they human, domestic or wild.

Though I had not yet been formally introduced to any reindeer I reasoned that any tracks I found that did not fit a cow, horse, antelope, badger, rabbit or weasel would have to be those of a reindeer.

Armed with all of that sign reading talent, I put on my rubber overshoes, bundled up in my sheepskin coat and donned my cap with rabbit fur ear flaps to venture out into the crisp air on that Christmas morning to apply my tracking skills to the Santa Claus problem. I stepped off the far end of the porch and started a slow transit around the outer perimeter of the front yard with my keen tracking eye looking for shadows in the snow which would indicate the presence of footprints. Uncle Happy had made sure that I learned never to wade into the middle of the area to be examined in such a careless and clumsy manner that your own footprints contaminate the clues for which you are searching.

I found paw prints of Gray Cat coming from the barn to the

front porch. I saw tracks of two mice that had come out of the coal house to survey the results of the winter storm. They evidently did not like what they saw as the mice had turned around to go back to the warmer climate of the coalhouse. Our resident bunny rabbit had emerged from his hiding place in the woodpile and hopped off to a haystack in the corral, probably in search of alfalfa leaves. But, to my surprise, I did not see any reindeer, sled or Santa Claus tracks.

The only answer to that puzzle was that Santa must have come along during the snowstorm so that all the tracks were covered up. It was evident that I would have to resort to more subtle examples of sign reading.

Animals almost always catch a piece or two of their hair on a fence barb, the limb on a tree or a nail head protruding from the barn. I concluded that Santa would have probably parked his reindeer at the end of the house where they might gain some respite from the storm. Therefore there was apt to be some reindeer hair stuck somewhere on the wall of the cabin. I found some cat hair stuck on a sliver of wood, probably caught there on one of Gray Cat's unsuccessful attempts to climb up to the roof. Threads of blue denim hung on a nail head left there from the arm of my jacket as I collided with the house one night during a hide-and-seek game. A lone porcupine quill lay on the ground next to the house indicating a visit by an animal that is no fun to pet. Nowhere did I find any reindeer hair.

My intense search was starting to give me a slight case of snow blindness so I decided to go back into the house to remedy that on-coming affliction with a cup of hot chocolate. As Mother handed me my chocolate she said, "Maybe Santa Claus landed on the roof and came down the chimney."

I could see the possibility of Santa Claus coming down one of those big stone chimneys into a fireplace which I had seen in pictures of houses in some far-off place called New England. I saw little chance that a roly-poly guy in a red suit would have any success coming down our chimney because it was made of metal and was only six inches in diameter. Furthermore, if he did get down the chimney he would fall right into a red-hot pile of coal smoldering away in a big pot-bellied stove to keep a modicum of heat in the cabin during the night. If nothing else, that would sure singe Santa's overshoes. I didn't think a smart person like Santa would try that trick.

The roof of our cabin presented some other pitfalls which I was sure that Santa Claus would be sure to avoid. The cabin was covered with corrugated, galvanized tin sheets which drained into eave-troughs to direct rain water or water from melting snow into an underground cistern. This was a splendid arrangement to collect water for washing but that tin roof was terribly slick with snow on it and I was sure Santa did not want to risk all his reindeer sliding off into a tangled heap in the yard.

A large pine tree was situated not far from our cabin from which seeds out of its ripening cones would drift down with passing breezes to settle on the tin roof of the ranch cabin. Various crows, magpies, meadowlarks and sparrows would take note of this tasty menu and descend upon the roof with knife and fork at the ready. You could hear the click-click of their talons on the tin as they walked around on the roof. When a flock of birds went to work on those coniferous morsels it sounded like a machine-gun war had broken out as their little beaks hit the tin roof in their frenzied efforts to pick up the pine nuts.

Gray Cat sat in the yard one day studying the bird convention on the roof and came to the conclusion that a feathered meal awaited him if he could find a way to get up there. After some analysis of the engineering factors involved, he solved that problem by climbing a wooden post, one of several supporting the front porch. There are not many places to hide on a tin roof when stalking game but Gray Cat finally learned to conceal himself behind the chimney until a bird carelessly got within leaping distance of him. Then Gray Cat would start his charge.

Gray Cat could accelerate from a crouch to a flying blur of fur in seconds on a surface into which he could dig his claws. You can guess how far he could dig his claws into a tin roof. The biggest hazard to the birds was that they might die of laughter as they watched Gray Cat spin his wheels trying to get up to speed on the tin roof. If you can't imagine what all that feline feather-chasing activity sounded like from inside the house, think of fingernails scratching on a chalkboard. It was enough to send cold chills up and down your spine and set your teeth on edge.

If a few birds and a cat could cause all that auditory fanfare on the roof, imagine the noise eight reindeer would make tromping around up there. I didn't even get the old wooden ladder to check out that idea.

My vision having been cured by the rich brew of chocolate, I decided to make one more search pattern through the yard just in case I had missed some small clue. As I reached for the handle on the squeaky door I heard Mother ask Dad, "Do you suppose we should tell Warren about—", and then her voice trailed off. I saw Dad shake his head, "No." Whatever it was that they weren't going to tell me must have been pretty serious stuff because both Mother and Dad had sad and somber faces as they watched me go out the door.

You have probably already guessed that my second tour of the yard was as unsuccessful as the first.

As I came back into the house, Wayne said in that infuriatingly smug way of his, "I know why you didn't find any Santa Claus tracks." I figured it was a little late to come up with any silly explanation he might have but I listened anyway as he continued, "Santa Claus has those little elves that sit on the back of his sled with little brooms and sweep out all the tracks." I was about to retort with my standard, "That's dumb." when I noted that Mother and Dad had big smiles on their faces. If such a silly idea could make them so happy it was not my place to ruin their fun. Besides, if I went along with that broom-wielding elf story, it gave me way to stop my search with my sign-reading reputation intact. So I shut up.

Additionally, my Santa tracking efforts had brought my parents perilously close totelling me something I wasn't so sure I wanted to hear, whatever it was.

TWENTY-SIX GATES

Because of barbed wire, I developed a liking for wieners and graham crackers at a fairly young age, a gastronomic delight which has stayed with me to the present day. Now that is a rare affliction for a young lad growing up on a Hereford cattle ranch where good beef-cuts were the entree *du jour* so let me lead you around the hills and through the pastures to see if I can explain that opening remark.

Fences of some kind have been around for a long time. The oldest and most spectacular fence in the world is the Great Wall of China. It is almost 2000 years old and consists of 2000 miles of stone forts and walls, along the top of which runs a protected roadway. The wall was originally built by Chinese military leaders having the misguided belief that it would stop attacks on China by unfriendly nomads from what is now Mongolia and Manchuria. Even though its original purpose was not fully achieved it has since led to another invasion of China by other humans, this time called tourists.

Kings and nobles ringed their castles with protective stone fences to which were added parapets and ramparts and, for the imaginative types, an encircling moat which was crossed only via a drawbridge. For a while, an entire section of the movie industry was devoted to the invasion of these types of fortifications by Errol Flynn types using grappling hooks and treachery.

While the Chinese Wall and the castle enclosures were built for protection against invading armies most fences of the world have been built by individuals to prevent domestic animals from straying into forbidden territory or out of their assigned areas.

I suppose one of the early reasons for putting up a fence was to keep your milk cow out of the garden where lettuce was like candy to that bovine species. The early settlers of the Thirteen Colonies probably fenced their small farms to keep their plow horse somewhere close to the barn instead of wandering off to get lost in the forest or, even worse, to stray over into the neighbors corn field thus prompting strong complaints from that otherwise friendly neighbor. And you sure wouldn't want the neighbor's horse wandering through your own corn field.

Most early fences were built by stacking the many inevitable stones that seem to grow in fields and gardens, or by cutting and trimming many small trees to provide the material to construct a pole fence. The use of stones or poles to build a fence around a garden or even a twelve acre farm required a lot of lifting and groaning but was not an impossible task. Someone must have noticed that farm animals tended to shy away from plants with sharp spiny spikes on their limbs because some fences were built by creating a hedge of blackberry bushes or other unfriendly plants. The natives of the desert Southwest built fences using the spiny stalks of the ocotillo (oka-tea-yo) for hundreds of years. These examples led several manufacturers to begin putting sharp spikes, called barbs, on strands of wire to make the first versions of barbed wire in the early 1800's.

Use of barbed wire to build a fence was a lot easier than heaving stones into a pile but the early products did not turn out to be very satisfactory because barbed wire was still expensive to purchase, corroded easily and often broke during the handling and bending which was part of the fence erection process. Nevertheless, there began a big demand for barbed wire when the United States Congress enacted the Homestead Act of 1862 which allowed a citizen to claim a quarter-section of land equal to 160 acres as his own for purposes of farming and the raising of farm animals. That was just too big a patch of land to allow serious consideration of piled stones or poles as a means of erecting an appropriate fence. Barbed wire thus became the material of choice to enclose a homestead despite its cost and technical deficiencies.

The 160 acre limitation on the original Homestead Act of 1862 began to receive some strong criticism from ranchers who filed for land in the blue sky country of Montana, the open plains of the Dakotas, and other real Western states. These hardy pioneers pointed out that it took about ten acres of sparse grassland to support one cow. They sure could not scare up a respectable trail drive with just sixteen cows.

After several years of lobbying by Western Senators, Congress finally amended the Homestead Act in 1916 to allow a person to claim an entire square mile of land, equal to 640 acres, for purposes of grazing livestock. This change in the law launched an enormous influx of homesteaders to the eligible western states with the result that most of the land available for filing was claimed by 1924. It also resulted in a fantastic demand for barbed wire with each homesteader now requiring four miles of fencing to enclose his claim.

Fortunately, by the 1900's, many improvements had been made in the quality and cost of barbed wire. An entrepreneur and inventor by the name of Joseph Farwell Glidden had noted the many problems with early barbed wire. In 1874 he obtained patents on changes he had made in the material used in the wire as well as the manufacturing process itself, both of which increased its durability and led to a decrease in customer cost. He modified the metallurgical structure of the component wires to make them more resistant to corrosion and breakage. Glidden made his production machines flatten the ends of the barbs and cut them at an angle so as to give them a sharper point which increased the respect for Glidden wire among animals chancing to encounter it in their travels. Almost all barbed wire made after that time used some or all of his patents and ideas.

At about the same time the Homestead Act was modified to allow 640 acre cattle grazing holdings in 1910, Dad rode his faithful saddle horse, Frosty, from the family farm in South Dakota over a couple hundred miles of southeastern Montana hills and valleys to go to work as a cowhand for the Leaf cattle spread west of Miles City, Montana. He participated in several cattle roundups and cattle drives for the Leaf outfit but, all the time he was touring the countryside on Frosty, he kept a sharp eye for terrain suitable for homesteading. He finally located a section of unclaimed land on Bowers Creek south of Broadus, Montana and filed on it in 1918. His choice was blessed with five natural springs for water, hills covered with pines from which he constructed a small log cabin, flatlands for farming and low creek beds providing wild grass hay. One side of Dad's homestead adjoined another already fenced but now Dad was in the market for six miles of barbed wire with which to fence the other three sides of his section of land. That six mile figure for the three sides comes about because a suitable fence consisted of a minimum of two strands of barbed wire.

When I was a youngster I did not think much about barbed wire fences—they were just there as a routine fact of my life. By that time, almost every piece of land around our ranch had been homesteaded and fenced. Then, when I was nine years old, Dad bought a new 1929 Chevrolet two-door sedan. That caused me to gain a new and startling awareness of fences and the necessary wire gates inserted on the wagon trails to allow passage from one pasture to another.

Prior to the advent of that Chevrolet sedan into our life, any traveling we did as a total family was in a wagon, buggy or, in the wintertime, a sled drawn by a team of horses. Mother and Dad sat up front on a spring-mounted double seat while my brother and I sat in the box bottom to the rear of my parents. When we came to a fence gate in this mode of travel, Dad would hand the reins to Mother, climb down from the seat, open the gate and let Mother drive the team and wagon through, close the gate and then climb back up on the seat to drive on down the wagon trail.

The introduction of the automobile led to a complete revision of the hierarchy of seating arrangements in the vehicle for our family; in fact, for all western families.

Anytime there was a passenger in a car in addition to the driver, that person became the designated gate-opener. If there was two or more passengers in two door sedan, the front-seat passenger was automatically chosen as the person to crawl out to open the gates. This choice becomes immediately clear when you think about the acrobatics required for a rear-seat passenger to exit and re-enter a two-door machine with someone already sitting in the front seat.

Mother could have sat in the front seat and opened the gates but that was an unseemly thing to have happen in those days, particularly when our family included a couple of young lads who could perform that task even though an extra-snug gate might create difficulties for a small frame. So Mother moved to the back seat of the sedan and my brother Wayne or I became the designated gate-openers with whichever of us was "off-duty" in the back seat with Mother.

This perfectly logical arrangement soon gave rise to an argument between Wayne and me as to who was to open the gates on a trip. After all, it was not a source of great fun to have to jump out of the car every half-mile or so to open one of those blasted gates. With a touch of Socratic wisdom, Dad decreed that he cared less as to who went first but that one of us would open the gates going and the other while we were coming back home. That seemed to settle that issue but I do remember, with very little remorse, smugly volunteering to be first on a sunny fall day knowing we would be returning home on a cold frosty evening in the darkness of night when it would be Wayne's turn at the gates.

Our ranch house was an even sixty miles from our "town," Gillette, Wyoming, so the trip was not made often. A trip to town was generally an all-day affair with our departure just after chores were done in the morning and a return after dark. That should not be surprising as there was five hours of travel time just to complete the 120 mile journey plus all of the business and visiting that adults took care of in town.

In the days of that 1929 Chevrolet, a trip to town created a marathon of gate opening. The first thirty miles of the route was originally a horse and wagon road into Gillette winding through the many ranches along the way. As a result, there were twenty six gates to town. The second thirty miles was completely free of gates athwart the road and completely fenced along the sides to keep animals off the highway. We could roar along the roadbed covered with red gravel at fantastic speeds sometimes as high as thirty-five miles per hour with a thrilling cloud of red dust rising behind us.

HOW TO READ A COW

That going and coming rule on gate duty assignments of Dad's worked pretty well on the town trips but it was soon modified by another perk that Dad threw into the equation.

Every young boy dreams of becoming a driver in one of Detroit's products thus giving him control of two tons of metal rushing down the highway. In furtherance of this dream, Dad would occasionally let the gate guy slide over next to him to shift gears as we pulled away from a gate stop or to steer the car on a long, straight stretch of road where any miscue would not have catastrophic results. It was not long after this practice was instituted that Wayne began volunteering to open gates on both directions of the trip thus enabling him to get more time at the wheel or gear shift lever. I was not at all that enamored with the dual driving lessons so I was not bothered a bit by my brother's insane desire to open 52 gates just to get a chance to wiggle the steering wheel for a few minutes.

While we were in town Mother would always buy fruits and foods we could not grow on the ranch or that she could not prepare herself. Thus it was that the pungent aroma of oranges or other fruit from far off places would waft through the car as we wended our way home in the dying hours of the day. Before long, I was able to con, coerce, or nag Mother into adding two other items to the list—wieners and graham crackers. Somehow the spicy smell of wieners rising from the meat counter in the grocery store had attracted my attention and I became an even greater fan of them after I got a chance to eat one. Dad's snide remarks describing the alleged unsavory contents of wieners did nothing to diminish my fondness for them. The sweet crunchy chewiness of graham crackers needs no explanation, even today.

My trip home was becoming downright pleasant. I would contentedly crawl into the back seat. When we were about ten miles out of town, Mother would hand me a raw wiener and a couple of graham crackers which I would munch with relish as the sagebrush flitted by. Then, if it was a cold day, I would snuggle into one of the ever present blankets and fall into a warm sleep. I thought it was rather dumb for my younger brother to put up with all those gates for a few brief interludes at the controls of the mechanical beast we were riding in although I was happy with the results for me.

I never have been able to understand how a person who was that dumb could later be one of the safest drivers I have ever ridden with, become the best auto mechanic in Montana, and a top car salesman in Billings.

YOU AREN'T OLD ENOUGH, YET

My parents developed a saying in our family which was to have a profound effect upon my life. I haven't quite figured out whether that effect was good or bad but it was profound. As a child, I would watch the adults around the ranch table smack their lips, go, "Ummmm!" and make all kinds of indecent sounds as they slurped their coffee after a big meal. I figured that anything that would cause that much emotional uproar in otherwise sane and staid adults must be pretty good stuff. But when I asked Mother if I could have some of that beautiful, steaming black liquid, she would shake her head from side to side and say, "You aren't old enough, yet."

It apparently took another 13 years before Mother decided I was old enough since she poured me my first cup of coffee on my 18th birthday. By then, I wasn't all that excited about the matter because I had snuck a few sips in the meantime and had decided that coffee just wasn't worth all the fuss it seemed to evoke in those adults. I later changed my mind but mainly because holding a hot cup of coffee in both hands seemed to brighten a cold and dark winter morning as one climbed out of the soogans.

That big Kalamazoo cook stove in Mother's kitchen required a considerable amount of wood to keep it stoked up to operating temperature particularly on special occasions like bean-canning time or Saturday night baths. That meant that the woodbox off the end of the kitchen had to be filled up on a fairly regular basis. That wood had to be transported from an enormous pile of split pine located at about the mid-point of the 250 feet between house and corral. One of my earliest memories is of Dad with an armload of wood headed for the house.

Though I now consider it a stupid move on my part, at three or four years of age I must have decided that filling the woodbox would sure be a fun, grown-up job. But when I made that proposal, Dad came up with, "You aren't old enough, yet." In defense of my parent's narrow minded approach on this matter, I can now accept the idea that they were probably trying to keep me from impaling myself on the sharp double-bitted axe which resided near the woodpile or to prevent me from being guillotined by the heavy woodbox cover. Be that as it may, my memory tells me that it was only a short span of time until I was old enough to transport the chopped wood.

Being the resourceful guy that I am, it soon became clear to me that I could improve the efficiency of that wood moving operation by employing certain modern equipment available to me. So I would take my little red wagon out by the woodpile, fill the box with wood, put one knee on top of the load and then scoot my way across that 125 feet to the house at the fantastic speed of 6 or 7 miles per hour. I even transformed the little red wagon into a heavy hauler by stacking one layer of wood sideways in the box to form a V shaped trough and then filled the V to the brim. If the draft door wasn't wide open on the Kalamazoo, I could transport a whole day's supply of wood in just a few loads.

Having successfully solved the logistics of wood transport, I looked around for bigger worlds to conquer. I began to pay more attention to the shiny double-bitted axe as Dad swung it toward a block of tree trunk with the objective of reducing it to sticks of wood like I had been hauling in my red wagon. There was a task with an element of skill to it and a hint of danger and excitement posed by that sharp blade. You guessed it, "You aren't old enough, yet." The verbal comma in that sentence left hope for a change of mind in the not too distant future.

I finally arrived at some age which Dad decided was "old enough" and I was called over to the woodpile and handed the axe. Dad took himself over to a tree stump and sat down far enough away to be out of harm's way and began to coach me on the finer points of splitting wood. That was when I learned my first dance steps, by the way. When your aim was a bit off and the axe ricocheted off the block of wood and headed for your foot you did some fancy stepping even if the orchestra wasn't playing a tune at the time. But, in a short time I was operating solo at the woodpile and, though not a real virtuoso with the axe, I still had five complete and attached toes in each shoe.

One day as I wiped the sweat from my brow and viewed, with some degree of pride, the large mountain of split wood I had produced there in the yard, I began to have a couple of niggling worries. I had noticed that Dad no longer carried wood to the woodbox. As I thought back further on the matter, it was also apparent to me that he had not split any wood for a long time. It was a terrible shock to me to realize that Dad was now so old that he could no longer fill the woodbox or split wood. That was particularly puzzling to me since Dad was in his mid-30's at the time. Concurrent with that worry came the thought that, unless I did something about it, I would be the only one filling the woodbox and splitting wood for the next several years. Just then my younger brother, Wayne, walked around the corner of the house.

I waved Wayne over by the woodpile and said to him, "I'll bet you will be glad when you are old enough to fill the woodbox, won't you?" I did not tell him that I had visions of him being old enough within the next five minutes.

He didn't hesitate a bit as he replied, "Nope." and then went down to the water pond by the corral and started throwing rocks at frogs. He evidently was considerably smarter than I was about that "You aren't old enough, yet" motivational speech—but he was a lot meaner to frogs.

Last summer, my wife and I visited a friend's ranch in Wyoming while we were on a vacation trip. Noting the large stock of unsplit wood they had gathered for their fireplace, I decided to be helpful by splitting some of those blocks into fireplace size. I noticed right away that it was a bit more difficult to get a stump up on the chopping block than I remembered from my younger years but stubborn pride pushed me onward for several hours until I had a big pile of split wood rising to the magnificent height of probably four inches.

The next morning getting out of bed seemed more complicated than usual. My shoulder hurt as if a horse had kicked me, I leaned to the south due to some vague lumbar dislocation and I had blisters on both hands. After I put my spectacles on, I did note with some degree of relief that I still had ten toes distributed equally and symmetrically on each foot.

My wife, who is a rather perceptive and sympathetic type, noted these symptoms of my honest toil from the day before and immediately changed my attitude toward the whole day to come by a few well-chosen words.

What she said was, "You darned fool, you're too old for that sort of thing."

WHAT A WALLOP

One of the more intellectual forms of entertainment in cow country was the perpetration of practical jokes on unsuspecting victims in the neighborhood.

Fred McNary, our closest ranch neighbor, had a formidable reputation as a practical jokester. I was privileged to witness the final act of one of his dramas one evening after other neighbors and I had spent a day helping Fred brand calves. We had saddled our horses and were sitting by the corral sipping cold spring water just before we all headed home to do chores when we noted a rider on a pinto horse meandering our way across Fred's lower pasture.

Fred had the eyesight of an eagle and after a second look in the direction of the oncoming rider he said with a chuckle, "I've been waiting three weeks for Jim to show up. Why don't you fellas hang around a bit." We didn't understand the reason for Fred's chuckle but decided milking time could wait as we settled down to see what Fred had in mind.

The rider wending his way up through the pasture was Jim Mueller, a bachelor rancher with a small spread located about three miles down Olmstead Creek from Fred's place.

Jim Mueller was moving our way rather slowly on his pinto horse so Fred used the time remaining until his arrival to describe his preparations for what we had now guessed was to be a practical joke on Jim.

About a month before our calf-branding activity, Fred was rooting around in a shed adjoining his chicken coop when he came across a box of dynamite. He had used part of the dynamite to blow rocks and stumps out of his alfalfa field and then had stored the remainder in a shed next to his chicken coop. He had forgotten about the dynamite but he sure paid close attention now that he had been reminded of its presence because the box appeared to be wet despite the fact that it had not rained for two weeks.

In those days, dynamite was made by soaking sawdust with nitroglycerin and then adding some glue to hold the mess together in a small cylindrical shape about a foot long. The nitroglycerin had a nasty habit of slowly seeping out of the sawdust to form puddles in the bottom of the container in which the dynamite was stored. The liquid form of nitroglycerin is a notoriously unstable substance which can be excited into exploding by a sharp impact such as dropping its container, be it box or bottle. Fred knew that an inquisitive cat or dog might knock that wet box of dynamite off its shelf with the probable result that he would have chicken feathers and wood splinters all over his yard. Fred made note of the fact that such an event would likely be injurious to the health and wellbeing of any cat or dog involved in such exploration.

Fred got a firm grasp on the dynamite box and then, with soft cat-like strides, carried it out of the shed, across the creek south of his corral and placed it at the foot of a big, dead pine tree about 100 yards away. He initially considered attaching a dynamite cap and fuse, as is done in normal use of dynamite, to torch off his little bomb. However, he decided it would do no harm where it was and might lend itself to education and amusement at a later date. That later date had arrived.

When it came to practical joking, Fred's attack on the unwary involved early selection of a specific victim, long and careful planning of the procedures to be used along with exquisite timing of its execution. The goal of some practitioners of the art was to anger or embarrass the victim but Fred's sole aim was to provide a laugh for himself, the spectators, and even sometimes the victim. It was this thoughtful and considerate approach to one of the favorite sports on the ranches of Wyoming which had gained Fred a reputation as a master jokester of northern Campbell County.

Anyone who failed to show the proper amount of humility about his skills, real or imagined, was a favorite target for Fred's pranks. Which brings us back to Jim Mueller.

Jim had a number of admirable skills including being an expert marksman with a rifle. He was always the first to get his deer in hunting season, or out of it, for that matter. He was the winner in local target shooting contests an annoying percentage of the time. He could have started a small war with the collection of rifles in his possession. We were glad he was basically a peaceable type in view of his considerable array of shooting tools.

Despite all of his fine attributes, Jim had one fault which wiped out any points he might have otherwise won in the ranching community. Modesty was a trait much admired by ranch people and Jim didn't have any. Most shooters, receiving a compliment on an accurate execution of a difficult shot would scuff the toe of their boot in the dust, bashfully hand his head, and say, "Just lucky, I guess." In the same situation, Jim would yell out for all to hear, "Look at that.

Right through the old bullseye." And it generally was.

Once Jim had ambled his pinto up to the corral and the "How-dies" and "Evenins" had been taken care of all around, Fred started pushing the proceedings along by remarking, "Looks like you have new rifle there, Jim." That remark prompted Jim to climb down from his horse and pull his rifle from the scabbard on his pinto's saddle and launch off on a collection of questionable statements about his new firearm. He claimed it would knock over a buffalo at 300 yards, had a flat trajectory up to 150 yards and then Jim spewed forth a bunch of fancy figures about muzzle velocity, shots per minute, and total cartridge magazine capacity. Thus was the battle joined between Fred and Jim.

Looking around as if to pick a suitable target, full well knowing which one he was going to suggest, Fred finally said to Jim, "Can you make out that cardboard box across the creek?" as he pointed in its approximate direction. Jim immediately recognized the veiled denigration of his visual acuity and retorted, "Sure can, if you mean that box with the red circle on its side sitting at the foot of that old pine tree across the creek"

Satisfied that he had Jim zeroed in on the desired target, Fred challenged, "That's it. If that little popgun of yours can shoot that far, see if you can put a hole right in the middle of that red circle."

Two insults in a row like that could not be ignored. Jim walked over to rest his gun on the top of nearby fence post, quickly aimed and pulled the trigger. A lot of surprising things happened immediately thereafter.

That old pine tree disappeared in a cloud of dust and flame with pieces of branches flying toward the sky. Leaves were completely stripped from nearby bushes to join the other debris. At least ten jackrabbits popped their heads above the sagebrush in a nearby pasture and loped away with their big ears flopping. Jim's pinto horse broke the reins wrapped around the hitching rail and galloped off behind the corral. Two deer bounded out of the trees and ran over the hill above Fred's house. A flock of chickens raised a complaining squawk and started running aimlessly around the barnyard. Every one of Fred's nine dogs started howling or barking and two of them ran to hide under the front porch. One of the spectators who was sitting on a one-legged milk stool tipped over backward into a pile of cow manure. All the rest of us jumped about a foot into the air. Through all of this, Jim did not even as much as blink an eye.

It was then that we knew we were witnessing a contest of epic proportions between an expert joker and a seasoned jokee.

Jim stood there at the fence post holding his gun until the reverberations of the dynamite blast had quit bouncing around the hills, the chickens had quit squawking and the dogs had ceased to bark. Then he patted the wooden stock of his weapon and said very quietly, "I knew this was a darn good rifle, but I didn't know it had that much of a wallop."

A NICKNAME IS BORN

One reason the big black gelding bronc acquired his name, Blackie, was because of his color. But he also had a dark personality that matched his name. He was a rather mean spirited beast with little respect for human beings and was determined that none of those two legged animals were going to stay on his back very long. Blackie was one of several broncs that Dad had purchased and farmed out to one of the local bronc experts to convert into reasonably trustworthy saddle horses. The bronc man succeeded quite well with all of the horses except Blackie. After six weeks of indoctrination, Blackie would still buck every time a rider got on his back and he was returned to the ranch, at no charge, with the snide suggestion that he be used for coyote bait.

Not long after Blackie was brought back to the ranch in a state of training limbo, a number of our neighbors gathered at our ranch house one hot summer Sunday. Our guests displayed proper respect for my mother's cooking by devouring several helpings of fried chicken, just-dug boiled potatoes with chicken gravy, whole wheat bread, wax string beans just out of the garden and other culinary delights topped off with home-made ice cream. The men then gathered on the shaded porch to pick their teeth and palaver a bit. After they had chewed on the subject of cattle prices for a while, reported on the grass conditions in their part of the country, and analyzed the energetic way in which Babe Peterson did the dosey doe at the Saturday night dance, the perplexing personality of Blackie came up for consideration.

One of the members of the toothpickin' club sitting on the porch was Eugene "Gene" Sorenson, a local single man in his mid-twenties with a reputation as a better-than-average bronc rider. Gene, although a pleasant and likeable guy, also had a reputation of being a bit cocky about his bronc riding abilities. When he heard of Blackie's stubborn reluctance to join the ranks of respectable saddle horsery, he allowed as how he would like to take a crack at changing Blackie's attitude. Several of the men, including Dad, immediately encouraged this thought, probably in the hope that Blackie would take the edge off some of Gene's cockiness by dumping him on the ground as he had done with all of the previous riders. Being the most junior person present, I was dispatched to bring Blackie from the horse pasture into a pine-pole corral which seemed to be the best available location for the forthcoming contest between Blackie and Gene.

Blackie gave no serious objection as Gene bridled him and put his own saddle on Blackie. That benign state of affairs changed as soon as Gene climbed into the saddle, though. Blackie immediately began a series of aerial gymnastics, each of which ended in a solid, four-footed landing of a type that jolts a rider's spine and tends to snap his hat off. However, true to his reputation, Gene stayed in the saddle through the best of Blackie's efforts in the middle of the corral—and even kept his hat on.

Now, that corral had one defect for a contest such as we were witnessing. It was built in a square shape with corners. The ideal shape for a bronc-busting corral is that of a circle with no corners. In a round corral, a horse will buck around the perimeter of the corral until the issue is settled one way or another. A square shape presents the possibility that a horse will buck along one side of the corral and then crash into the adjacent side because he cannot make the turn. Blackie did not do any stupid, clumsy thing like that but he did, apparently, decide to use the corner for a time-out to reconsider his options. He bucked along one side of the corral and then stopped with his head in the corner and a thoughtful look on his long face.

Gene tried to encourage Blackie to come out of that corral corner and fight like a horse by judicious application of spurs and the ends of his leather bridle reins to various parts of Blackie's anatomy. Blackie continued to stand with his head in the corner with a rather sullen look on his face. In exasperation, Gene applied the ultimate insult and attention-getter to Blackie—he reached forward, grabbed Blackie's left ear and twisted rather energetically. In a flash, Blackie brought his head out of the corner and reached around to sink his teeth solidly into Gene's left calf. That induced Gene to bail out of the saddle to climb over the pole fence and fall, white-faced, into the adjacent hay corral. It was almost a certainty that Blackie had won Round Two.

It was soon evident that Gene was in a bit of trouble. Blackie's bite had torn loose a large chunk of muscle from Gene's calf with the wound bleeding quite profusely. In addition, there was some indication that the uncontrolled fall from the pole fence might have fractured his left ankle. The nearest doctor was 60 country miles away and nobody in attendance that Sunday owned a Model T Ford or a reasonable facsimile thereof. Any serious medical attention would require a 25 mile buggy trip to the home of a rancher who had an automobile with which to finish the journey to the doctor's office. After some applied first-aid, that is the mode of transportation which eventually prevailed. Gene's wounds received a liberal application of iodine and some embroidery work by the town doctor and he was soon back trying to coerce horses to the ways and mores of man.

But let us back up to the scene where Gene is lying in the hay corral with a forkful of alfalfa for a pillow with everybody realizing that he may have some fairly serious injuries. Rural humor was often used to diffuse an unpleasant situation and this incident proved to be no exception. Dad took a look at Gene and evidently deciding he was going to live, said, "If you had been wearing a piece of stovepipe, Blackie wouldn't have been able to get a grip on you". That remark got a pretty good laugh from the assembled group with the possible exception of the bleeding victim.

For the next 15 years that I was around the country, Gene was known as Stovepipe Sorenson! Another change came over Gene after his encounter with Blackie, which improved his standing in the community. He displayed considerably more humility about his bronc riding skills than he did on that fateful Sunday afternoon when he met up with Blackie.

Blackie? Dad discovered that he would tolerate a harness without strenuous complaint with the result that Blackie spent the rest of his working life pulling heavy farm machinery.

BIB OVERALLS

Bib overalls looked like they belonged on an engineer of a steam locomotive back in the 1920's and, along with a cap of the same tough denim material, became a uniform for that profession. While ready to look with admiration and envy upon a railroad engineer wearing bib overalls, the budding young cow hands of that era were adamantly opposed to wearing bib overalls themselves. My animosity toward being clothed in bib overalls was prompted by my opinion that they did not fit the sartorial image of a cow hand, were a hazard to the safety of life and limb when you were around oscillating animals and machinery and were an invitation to disaster should you have to make an urgent visit to the privy on a cold winter day.

Had we been given our choice of wardrobe, my friends and I would have been decked out in form fitting, narrow legged pants requiring a wide leather belt with a silver buckle into which would be tucked a shirt tailored with a rib-hugging taper cut. Naturally, we would have stomped around in high-heeled Western leather boots with our initials embossed on the sides. All of this finery would be topped off with a tan Stetson sporting a hat-band made of rattlesnake skin—with the rattles still attached. With such a costume, I would have been able to sit tall in the saddle, particularly when my pretty city cousin, Eilene, came out to the ranch to visit. As it turned out, I had to hunker down pretty low to the saddle in bib overalls when she and her friends came around.

However, our unwillingness to willingly accept having our bodies draped with bib overalls did us no good since parents made that abominable costume the universal choice of attire for me and my young male friends as we were growing up on the ranches of northeastern Wyoming.

In defense of my parents bull-headed attitude in favor of clothing me in bib overalls, I must admit that the tough blue denim from which they were made would take considerable abuse before any part of my anatomy started to show through in a seriously embarrassing way. I probably should give credit to bib overalls for minimizing damage to my epidermis during my numerous encounters with barbed wire, cactus, sharp rocks, hay rakes and temperamental animals during the early part of my ranching career. I suppose they were more economical to buy for us than the snug belted pants we really wanted.

In an effort to stretch that dollar even further, Mother would send off a mail-order to Sears and Roebuck for bib overalls two or three sizes too big for me. In my opinion, this was a blatant violation of sensible sartorial planning but Mother knew that I would soon outgrow the garment if she ordered the size that would fit my growing frame at the time of purchase. This practice no doubt saved my parents some money but it sure caused a lot of physical and mental trauma for me.

Once the mailman had delivered the Sears package with those monstrously oversized new bib overalls, I was faced with a making a number of adjustments and modifications to them. The suspenders had slip buckles so that you could adjust the length of the suspenders and after a few trials I could get the upper part of the garment to fit my short torso with some degree of comfort. However, after a few months of growth engendered by age and my Mother's fine cooking, those bib overalls would begin to fit a bit tight at the crotch and I would have to slide the adjusting buckles to a new position to alleviate the developing pain and discomfort. I don't think this phenomenon is classed among what are called growing pains, but it sure was one.

The leg length on those oversized bib overalls presented an adjustment challenge of a different nature. Even after you had snugged up the suspenders to a point just short of bodily injury, the pant legs would still be long enough to drag in the cow manure should you be so stupid as to go sashaying around the corral prior to further modifications. Knowing that such a stupid move would incur Mother's wrath as well as generating considerable olfactory displeasure for nearby citizens when you later sat by the warm, pot-bellied stove, I made the necessary changes in the pant legs. This procedure was not very complicated. I just turned them up into a cuff, sometimes taking two turns to get them up to a level which would preclude contamination by the surprises found lying on the ground around a ranch. As I was to learn, this cuff creation solved one difficulty but created several others.

As you perform a number of chores around a ranch you come into close proximity to a number of animals. Such intimacy with bovine animals occurs at milking time, when you are distributing hay and grain to the calves, or when you are wrestling a calf at branding time. As you probably know, the hoof of a younger member of the cattle species is fairly small. In fact, it is just about the right size to fit inside the rolled up cuff on a pair of too-big bib overalls. You know one of the animals has played the old foot-in-the-cuff game on you when the suspenders on that loathsome garment cuts a groove about two inches deep into your shoulders. No doubt this double stab of pain will gain your immediate attention but, if not, the animal will soon remedy that omission by stepping on your foot as the two of you begin a lock-step dance around the corral. As a youngster, I had little choice but to dance with the animal because he generally out-weighed me, two or three to one.

Even if I managed to stay off the dance program of my bovine friend, the cuffs on those bib overalls were waiting to set off another time bomb in my face should I be the least bit neglectful of their ominous presence.

One evening after a particularly grueling day about the ranch, I came into the cabin and sat down on a chair in the corner of the kitchen to take off my work boots before getting ready for supper. As anyone might normally do, I put one foot up on the opposite knee so I could undo the laces on my weary footwear. As I did so a surprising collection of debris began to fall out of the cuffs of my bib overalls to litter Mother's spotless kitchen floor. A plentiful supply of sand and clods of dirt first fell to the floor. I had apparently collected these as I plodded along behind a spring-toothed drag in a field that day. Two live grasshoppers jumped out of the cuff but quickly disappeared by hopping across the room to a hiding place under the kitchen stove. I had dropped two machine bolt nuts while I was adjusting a seat on the corn cultivator and I now knew where they had magically hidden themselves. One of the horses must have gotten a short ration of oats that evening as I fed the team since there was now enough oats on the kitchen floor to plant an acre of ground. Mother's glaring look in my direction fortified my distaste for bib overalls but that did not seem to be an opportune time to again bring up that opinion with her.

As a result of that cuff dumping incident, Mother stopped giving me a friendly greeting when I came in from my toils. Her opening remark changed to a somewhat stern, "Did you empty your cuffs before you came in?"

The injury to my cowhand image by being forced to wear bib overalls was bad enough. The continual adjustments required as my size increased was troublesome. The unwelcome terpsichorean contest with a young heifer was often painful. The debris collection in the cuffs decreased my social standing around the house. But all of those liabilities paled when compared to the depredations which could be perpetrated by the bib section of those disgusting bib overalls.

After adjusting the suspenders and rolling in some cuffs on a pair of bib overalls just arrived from Sears you were still left with the bib section flopping around loosely in the wind. All that extra blue denim material of the bib was an open invitation to snagging on plow handles, horns of irritated bulls, plum tree limbs, or protruding nails.

Take the matter of getting on an energetic saddle horse where timing and smooth motion have a great deal to do with successful completion of that operation. Adults could easily accomplish this critical maneuver by putting a foot in the left stirrup, grabbing the saddle horn and then quickly planting themselves firmly in the saddle. Being considerably smaller than an adult, I had to resort to a different procedure mainly consisting of crawling and slithering up the side of the animal. All too often, this ungainly journey resulted in the saddle horn inserting itself into the bib section of that dangerous article of clothing. At that very instant, the horse would start dancing around with the result that my foot would slip out of the stirrup. It immediately became apparent that should I abandon my upward transit in favor of a new start that I was headed for a very painful side-saddle ride. With that inducement, I was generally able, somehow, to claw my way to the top of the animal.

I am not even going to tell you the horrible details of that urgent trip to the outdoor privy on a cold day when you discover that the suspenders are trapped under your heavy winter jacket.

COW COUNTRY FUNERAL

Ben Reader keeled over in his horse corral and died in late August of 1929. A neighbor who had delivered a bull to Ben's ranch discovered Ben lying supine in his corral. There being no close by coroner, the local postmaster decreed that Ben had died because his heart had just quit pumping. He so stated in the paperwork he sent off to the county seat in Broadus Montana.

Ben joined the Big Roundup in the Sky in a manner he would probably have picked had he been given a choice.

Word of Ben's demise soon spread and by noon of the next day several dozen members of neighboring families had gathered at the Reader ranch house to participate in a rural funeral. They came by wagon, buggy, and on horseback bringing with them a varied collection of roast beef, fried chicken, bread, cakes, cookies and other culinary goodies with which the women would put together a midday meal. My family members and I had arrived by team and wagon with a crock of Mother's renowned oatmeal cookies and a burlap sack of sweet corn. For these folks, a funeral, prairie fire, or an earthquake was a handy excuse to turn the affair into a social gathering with a good meal.

HOW TO READ A COW

Lest you think the gathered crowd was trying to get Ben into the ground with a bit too much haste, let me remind you that it was a hot summer day with no refrigeration available. Old Ben smelled bad enough when he was alive and any undue delay in funeral proceedings for him was certain to make matters worse. To minimize that problem, the amateur undertakers had placed Ben's remains in a cool dugout located back of Ben's two-story house.

Ben had been a cattle rancher in Powder River County of southern Montana. His ranch was three miles north of the Montana Wyoming border and twenty miles west of Little Powder River.

Ben was a short, bow-legged widower with so many creases and wrinkles on his face that it was difficult to judge his age. Though he had been ranching in the area for at least eighteen years, he had not told anyone much about his background. No one could recall Ben mentioning his birth date. Many of his neighbors guessed his age to be in the early seventies. So Ben's death was not untimely—just sudden.

Perhaps Ben's reluctance to talk about his background was the prevailing rumor in the ranching community that he had participated in an armed robbery of the Belle Fourche, South Dakota, Butte County Bank in 1897. The passage of time and history's examination of the facts started a replacement rumor that Butch Cassidy and the Sundance Kid did the 1897 bank robbery. Sundance did steal a horse from a South Dakota rancher named John Clay to start his criminal career. John Clay just happened to be part owner of the Butte County Bank.

Actually, Sundance along with George Currie, Kid Curry, Walt Punteney, and Tom O'Day participated in the robbery of the Butte County Bank. The robbery of the bank and the follow-up by the law was a comedy of errors. O'day was arrested hiding in a privy behind a local saloon after O'Day's horse decided to leave town without O'Day. Walt Punteney is generally credited as being the last surviving member of the Wild Bunch, having died on April 19, 1950, in Pinedale, Wyoming.

Back at Ben's funeral preparations, the wood working experts planning Ben's casket or coffin did not have access to a neatly varnished walnut casket with shiny handles and decorative metal pieces mounted on its sides. Instead, they began creating a casket from wood available around the house and corral of Ben's place. The best wood for this purpose came from a small shed near Ben's dugout. It had a fair collection of straight boards that had turned gray from many years of exposure to the sun and occasional rain. After the carpenters had demolished the shed, the young lads of the crowd got to participate in the building of Ben's final resting enclosure. They were assigned the task of removing and straightening the nails from the lumber of the old shed as the men finished their cups of coffee with pie after dinner.

In a short time, the funeral experts had created a gray casket and placed it in the box of a wooden wheeled wagon they located in the ranch barn. This was the conveyance that would transport Old Ben to the rural graveyard four miles down Bowers Creek to the east of Ben's cattle ranch. The wagon sides were made up of lumber also colored gray by the Montana weather elements so the casket and wagon presented a neat and attractive rural version of a hearse.

It was time to fetch Ben's body from the dugout and place it into the gray casket. This was accomplished with as much tender care as could be dredged up from the sweaty undertakers. As they began to nail down the gray cover on the amazingly solid box a couple of the straightened nails we had produced bent over double. Evidently one of us young lads had not done a very good job of straightening his nails, or they had hit a pine knot when they were driven into the wood.

After hooking a visiting team's tugs to the double trees of the hearse, the driver was ready to begin the slow trek to Ben's final resting place. Ten or twelve wagons and buggies with their passengers made up the rest of the entourage following the hearse. Saddle horse riders were in flank position to the wagons with two of them rushing ahead to open the barbed wire gates on the route so the procession could pass through without halting.

In later years, I observed several city type funeral affairs made up of a big black Lincoln Continental hearse carrying the guest of honor followed by 20 or 30 automobiles of attending friends and relatives of the deceased. Three or four local policeman on motorcycles would escort this procession and rush ahead of the long line of cars to stop traffic at intersections then repeat that operation for the next intersection.

There were no motorcycles handy for Ben's procession of wagons and buggies so riders on saddle horses substituted for the local policeman and rushed ahead of the line to open gates in the wire fences through which the train had to pass through. I continue to be amazed by the similarity of human actions in response to events that take place over widely separated decades of time.

After about an hour and a half of sedate travel, we finally reached the rural graveyard. Even at nine years of age, several thoughts immediately ran through my brain pertaining to the graveyard.

The graveyard was located on the top of a small knoll in one of Dean Mateur's cow pastures. It sure was not any good for growing thick grass for livestock so I could see why it was chosen in cow country. When I looked down in the excavation prepared for Ben, I noted that there were no rocks in the soil so it had to be easy digging in the sandy loam I could see lining the edges. It was not placed in a grassy creek bed for obvious reasons having to do with running water during a heavy rainstorm.

Like the missing coroner, there was no preacher to officiate when it came to speechifying time over Ben's gray coffin. As a substitute for that endeavor, a local county commissioner, Bruce Johnson, probably exaggerating a bit, made a ten minute speech about the fine and upstanding personality of Ben, mixed with Amens and mumblings of the surrounding parishioners.

I also noted that the saddle ropes that they used to lower Ben and the gray box into the ground were pulled out from under the casket, neatly coiled and strapped to the pommels of the owner's saddle.

As the wagons departed the graveyard with their passengers, some went east toward Little Powder River. The remainder retraced the route back up Bowers Creek to Ben's ranch and then onward to their own ranches.

We had used up most of the hours of the day doing the things we needed to do to get Old Ben buried so it was nigh on milking time. As I rode along in the back of our wagon I recalled one aspect of the funeral proceedings that emphasized the sensitivity of the rope handlers to matters of local economy.

They did not do anything so silly as to throw the loose ends of their ropes down into the grave to be covered up with six feet of dirt thus destroying two good saddle ropes. Instead, they neatly extracted the ropes from under Ben's coffin and strapped them to their saddles.

Had it not been such a somber occasion, the onlookers would have probably given the rope handlers a round of applause.

PUT YOUR LITTLE FOOT

Henry Colgan produced a respectable beat on the drums he played at the dance held every Saturday night in the summer time at Hunter's Dance Hall. Margaret Colgan, Henry's wife, played piano with her synchronized tinkling of the black and white keys. Their son, Jeffrey Colgan, stayed with the rhythm set by Henry and Margaret but he would hit an occasional note on his violin that sounded like it belonged in another song. The dancers did not break stride as they sashayed around the floor despite the musical didoes of Jeffrey.

Margaret was the postmistress of the Bay Horse, Montana post office so she collected some government money for that duty. The Colgans had a collection of white faced Hereford cattle so playing dance music was not required for them to buy flour and sugar. However, they did not refuse the coins and bills collected in a big Western style hat during the evening intermission at about 10:00 pm.

The dance hall activity changed dramatically at midnight. All of the dancing ranchers never went more than six hours between meals and the last one they had eaten was near six the previous evening. So, come midnight, the dancing stopped and some of the women crowded into an anteroom to the dance area and began preparing food while men went outside to have a swallow or two of booze or smoke a cigarette. Perhaps the brave types would choke down some chokecherry wine right from the bottle.

There were always several potato salads each invented by some ethnic group, most often German. A big pan of beans decorated another table largely because it was easy to prepare and transport without refrigeration. A big basket of fried chicken was always popular at the dances. Dessert consisted of cakes and pies fabricated by attending rancher wives.

The most spectacular container was a large shiny copper boiler sitting on top of a big cooking range going full blast with its fuel of pitch filled wood. It contained about ten gallons of water and a bag of ground coffee. The ensuing aromatic air would soon waft throughout the entire building to the delight of coffee drinkers.

No such thing as a "baby sitter" existed in the days of that period almost before automobiles. As a result, there were a number of children dispersed around the benches which adorned three walls of the dance hall while the adults did their dosey doe. But, during the midnight dance hiatus by adults, the dance floor was taken over by kids running and trying to slide as far as their momentum would propel them. Children played a maddening game called "Crack the Whip" which caused the child at the end of the line to go spinning off from the group at a high rate of speed. The kids performed these athletic affairs between trips to the door of the kitchen anteroom to ask for another cookie.

I got to remain in the dance hall while the adults, including my father, danced one more waltz or foxtrot and then it was out to the wagon where I would sleep while the adults danced on until daybreak. By that time I was tired and ready to go to bed. My father had put ten inches of straw and some warm blankets in the wagon bed and I welcomed climbing into them.

As I lay there on my makeshift bed in the wagon I could faintly hear the Coogans starting up another tune and I could imagine the skill and grace my father would be dancing a waltz or foxtrot inside the hall.

As I nodded off to sleep I could hear the lyrics and the associated tune I can still remember today, like the following:

PUT YOUR LITTLE FOOT

Put your little foot, put your little foot,

put your little foot right there;

Put your little foot, put your little foot,

put your little foot right there.

Take a step to the right, take a step to the left;

Take a step to the rear, but forever stay near.

Put your little foot, put your little foot,

put your little foot right there;

Put your little foot, put your little foot,

put your little foot right there.

CUT HIM LOOSE

I have a weakness for western movies particularly if they are oldie-goldies resurrected on television with John Wayne, Henry Fonda, or Walter Brennan. Even if the plot is weak, there is always a great display of beautiful scenery, handsome horses, and at least one good looking woman—not necessarily in that order.

The hero, naturally played by John Wayne, comes upon a group of nefarious characters about to hang Herb, whose only mistake involves being a sheep herder. Herb has his hands tied behind him and is sitting backwards on a horse with a noose already around his neck with the rope already thrown over the large limb of a big spruce tree which just happens to be conveniently available. Jake, the bad guy leader, is about to slap Herb's horse on the rump which will not hurt the horse but will cause considerable consternation for Herb, as the hero gallops into the scene.

First there is a long and loud palaver between John Wayne and Jake with accompanying close-ups of grimaces and steely-eyed looks between the two. The second possibility is that one of the bad guys decides to do John Wayne in and goes for his gun. Inevitably, the hero is always the faster draw artist with the demise of the foolish bad guy providing a fine incentive for restraint by the nine other bad guys still sitting on their horses. In either case, the hero then says, "Cut him loose." That is when I start to cry.

Most of the time, nobody carries a "hangin rope" around with them—even in those days. What they used was one of the ropes they carried on their saddles as a normal tool of their trade—which generally had to do with cattle. That rope was normally used to capture their horse du jour out of the remuda, to overcome the reluctance of a calf to willingly submit to a hot branding iron and loss of his testicles, or to encourage a recalcitrant cow to come out of the brush she was trying to hide in.

Coming by a good saddle rope was a rather exacting task. The first obstacle was cost. You generally packed about 50 feet of one-half inch rope neatly coiled up and attached to your saddle with a strap provided for that purpose on the pommel of your rig. Now, even if you use ten cents per foot as a purchase unit cost, you already had a $5.00 investment—lots more today. What you got for that was just straight rope.

To convert that piece of rope into a useful tool, you had to put a "honda," into one end of it. If you were sloppy and careless you might just put some kind of a knot out there to make a small loop—but that knot became very rough on the fingers when you used the assembly. The best way to form the honda was to braid the end of the rope back into the body so as to form a narrow and smooth oval. That could take a couple of hours to do correctly.

If you were to put the unit into service at this stage, it would not be long before the dally end would unravel or fray. So you had to braid that end as well, or wrap it with fine rawhide string.

Before you had a useful saddle rope, you had a fair investment and a lot of work into the thing.

Even though the rope probably belonged to one of the bad guys it would have been a lot more practical to just loosen the noose, slip it off Herb's head, neatly coil the rope and present it to him as a memento of the day's activities. But, no—John Wayne says, "Cut him loose." And there goes another good saddle rope.

ABOUT THE AUTHOR

Warren Hunt was born in 1920 in South Dakota. He and his mother soon made the trip from his birthplace to his parents' ranch, where he grew up as a cow hand. He attended the South Dakota School of Mines and then entered a long career in the then young airline field. As a Communications Director for Pacific Northern Airlines and later for Mohawk Airlines, he spent a lot of years with his feet off the ground. Before retiring, he taught electronics in upstate New York. He now resides near his children in Kent, Washington.

warrenhunt7@comcast.net

HOW TO READ A COW

WARREN V. HUNT

Made in the USA
San Bernardino, CA
16 November 2016